The Mighty Tortoise

Jane Williams has taught theology at Trinity College, Bristol, and is presently a lecturer at St Paul's Theological Centre, Visiting Lecturer at King's College London, and Anglican Editor at Redemptionist Publications. A regular contributor to the *Church Times*, she is married to Rowan Williams, the Archbishop of Canterbury.

Church Times Study Guide

The Mighty Tortoise

Exploring the Church

Jane Williams

CANTERBURY
PRESS
Norwich

© Jane Williams 2006

First published in 2006 by the Canterbury Press Norwich
(a publishing imprint of Hymns Ancient & Modern Limited,
a registered charity)
9–17 St Alban's Place, London N1 0NX

www.scm-canterburypress.co.uk

British Library Cataloguing in Publication data

A catalogue record for this book is available
from the British Library

ISBN 1-85311-715-3/978-1-85311-715-2

Typeset by Regent Typesetting, London
Printed and bound by Gallpen Colour Print,
Norwich 01603 624893

Contents

1

What's in a Name?

'Like a mighty tortoise moves the church of God/ Brothers, we are treading where we've always trod' goes the parody. It can be sung to the tune of 'Onward, Christian Soldiers', and it assumes that if the Christian soldiers of the Church are actually marching at all, it is simply on the spot, and the chances are that we will march so long and so hard on this one spot that eventually we shall go through, fall into a black hole and disappear from view altogether, and that will be no great loss.

In other words, the parody assumes that it is a bad thing to be treading where we have always trod. And that, in turn, suggests that the author of the parody had some clear ideas of what a church should be like. It should be active, it should be moving forward, it should be more like the Christian soldiers of the hymn whose tune it uses, and march off to war.

But others might disagree. They might want to argue that treading where it has always trod is precisely what the Church should be doing, since the Church is not a political or social movement but the society of those called into relationship with the eternal God. Where else would it be moving to?

The word 'church' would lend itself to the latter interpretation of the role. It comes from the Greek *kurikon*, meaning 'belonging to the Lord', and implies that the most basic characteristic of the Christian church is that we belong to the Lord Jesus. While few would dispute that, it isn't the word that the earliest church used to describe themselves, and it probably needs unpacking a little, if it is to be anything but a pious platitude.

New Testament Christians seem to have described themselves using either the familiar word 'synagogue', which simply means 'a gathering'; or *ekklesia*, which, literally translated, means 'called out', but was also used quite generally to mean 'an assembly of people'. Both the book of Acts and the letters of St Paul suggest that the first Christian gatherings were very much modelled on the synagogues that would have been familiar to the first Christians. Whenever Paul visits a new place, he starts off at the local synagogue, where he knows he will meet people who read the scriptures, believe in one God, and will be able to engage with the message of Jesus the Messiah, even if they do not agree with him. As time went on, more and more new Christians had no Jewish background and Paul seems to have been at the forefront of the battle not to make non-Jewish converts follow Jewish regulations about food and circumcision. It is not entirely clear whether it was Jews or Christians who insisted on the formal separation between the two communities, but by the time that it is really clear that Christians are not just a sect within Judaism, this synagogue pattern of meeting was probably quite deeply imbued in the Christian community.

Like the synagogues, Christians had a weekly pattern, with one day of the week as a special day. For Jews, it was the Sabbath, and for Christians it became the first day of the week, the day of the Resurrection. But these Christian synagogues, like their Jewish counterpart, were much more than just places where the faithful met once a week for worship. In the days before state-provided schooling or welfare systems, the Christian community would have provided scripture teaching, classes on Christian behaviour, food for the poor, and systems for settling disputes. Acts shows us some of these in operation.

Acts 2.42–7 gives what is undoubtedly a slightly idealized picture of the earliest converts:

> They devoted themselves to the apostles' teaching and fellowship, to the breaking of bread and the prayers.
>
> Awe came upon everyone, because many wonders and signs were being done by the apostles. All who believed were together and had all things in common; they would sell their possessions and goods and distribute the proceeds to all, as any had need. Day by day, as they spent much time together in the temple, they broke bread at home and ate their food with glad and generous hearts, praising God and having the goodwill of all the people.

- Notice the several different activities involved for these early Jerusalem-based Christians: there were specifically Christian things, like teaching from the apostles and breaking bread, but also continuing Jewish observance at the temple, where the Christians may well have gathered in a distinctive group, but still seeing themselves as part of the Jewish community.
- It is hard to tell just how much time these Christians spent together. Presumably, they cannot all have lived together, but it does sound as though they ate together regularly, and the ones with jobs and money supported the ones without. We see this aspect again in Acts 6. There are now too many converts for the apostles both to teach and to administer the practicalities, so they appoint seven men to distribute the food and see that everyone is fairly treated.

Acts 5, Acts 9, Acts 11 and Acts 21 show the Christian community, particularly its recognized leaders, acting as a kind of legal system, or a court for settling disputes:

- Acts 5 shows a couple who weren't quite ready to share all their goods with the rest of the community. For their deceitfulness, Peter condemns them and they drop dead. Not all such gatherings had quite such dramatic outcomes!
- When Saul is converted and becomes Paul, he goes up to Jerusalem and has to be vetted by the Jerusalem Christians before his ministry can be accepted, according to Acts 9. (He tells this story slightly differently in Galatians 1, so as to get rid of the impression that his ministry had to be vetted by anyone but God.)
- In Acts 11, Peter goes to the Jerusalem community to explain why he has just baptized a Roman centurion and his family, without any of the necessary Jewish preliminaries.
- Acts 21 continues that discussion about the terms on which non-Jews can be admitted to the Christian community, this time in the context of Paul's extraordinarily successful Gentile missions. Again, Paul and his companions bring their case to Jerusalem.

Although this pattern might suggest that it was only the Jerusalem community that could act as arbiters of Christian life, Paul's letters suggest that that was a feature of Christian gatherings in all the churches that he helped to found. They meet to hear teaching, they meet to break bread and eat together, they meet for worship, and they meet to debate issues regarding their life together, including disciplinary problems, when necessary. Paul is very shocked to hear from one of his churches that some Christians are choosing to pursue lawsuits in front of non-Christians, rather than settling matters within the fellowship of believers (see 1 Corinthians 6.1–7). He does expect the churches that he has founded to appeal to him on occasions, when they just cannot decide for themselves, and he expects all the Christian communities to care about each others' welfare. They are not independent congregations. They are united, but just happen to live in different places. The lists of greetings at the end of many of Paul's letters show that Christians did travel about quite a bit, and expected to be welcomed by the Christian community wherever they went.

Summary

The early Christian communities that we see in the New Testament met for teaching, for worship, for meals, and for disciplinary purposes. They had a common purse for the welfare of the poorer members of the community. They were a centre for learning how to live as Christians, day by day and in the whole of life, not just 'in church', which is not a phrase that they would have understood at all.

Exercise

1 Most parish churches nowadays have a 'mission statement'. Find out if yours does, and if so, look at it. It describes what that community thinks it is for and what it is trying to do.
2 If a sympathetic but uninvolved observer had to describe the purpose of the Church from what they have seen, what do you think they would say?

2

The Body of Christ

Although our investigations of the New Testament church suggest that there is an element of pragmatism and serendipity in the way in which the first Christians organized their lives together, there was also a great deal of theology. Very few religions are designed to be practised alone. Nearly all involve a corporate element. But for Christians this is not just a useful way of passing on information and support, but a way of being that shows what we are supposed to be for. The way in which Christians live together is part of the message. Church is part of gospel.

So a lot of early Christian literature, including the New Testament, is designed to facilitate 'church', that is 'belonging to the Lord'. It is designed for worship, exhortation, instruction, encouragement. It is the letter writers of the early church who reflect most openly about what the community of believers should be like and what best describes them. The letters of John talk about love as the most characteristic attribute of the Christian, because it is the most characteristic attribute of the God whose family we have become. John calls believers God's 'little children', signifying not just our dependence and ignorance, but also our entry into a new race, with new loyalties and new family ties. This is an idea picked up in 1 Peter as well. Peter tells the community, 'You are a chosen race, a royal priesthood, a holy nation, God's own people' (1 Peter 2.9).

Characteristically, it is Paul who provides one of the central definitions of 'church', which pulls together and focuses many of the ideas found elsewhere in the New Testament. Although Paul does not use the phrase 'body of Christ' very often, it makes sense of so many other things that he says about what it is to be 'church'.

Dead yet living

The church is full of 'dead men walking', according to Paul. All of us have chosen the death of one way of life in us so that Christ's new way of life can be born in us. That is what our baptism symbolizes, and why baptism is the way of Christian initiation. It chooses death so that we can live.

> Do you not know that all of us who have been baptized into Christ Jesus were baptized into his death? Therefore we have been buried with him by baptism into death, so that just as Christ was raised from the dead by the glory of the Father, so we too might walk in newness of life. (Romans 6.3–4)

> Paul is very much aware that the death of the old life in us is partial, but he is convinced that the process is none the less real for that. This language is partly metaphorical and partly sacramental – it begins to achieve what it utters.

The life of the Spirit

One of the results of the blossoming death of our old life is that we are no longer bound by our sins. Although we do still sin, that is dealt with by Jesus, along with our old life. Romans 8 is an extraordinarily difficult and profound exploration of what it means for us to be 'in Christ'. One of the most significant things Paul says is that our incorporation into Christ means that we are now animated by God's own life force, the Holy Spirit.

> There is therefore now no condemnation for those who are in Christ Jesus. For the law of the Spirit of life in Christ Jesus has set you free from the law of sin and death . . . But you are not in the flesh; you are in the Spirit, since the Spirit of God dwells in you . . . When we cry, 'Abba! Father!' it is that very Spirit bearing witness with out spirit that we are children of God, and if children, then heirs, heirs of God and joint heirs with Christ. (Romans 8.1, 9, 15–17)

The life of God being lived in us is not something we achieve by sheer will power, but by the presence of the Holy Spirit. We do not suddenly become good, but we are able to stand in what Luther called 'borrowed righteousness', wearing the goodness that is Christ's. Colossians 1.21–2 says 'And you who were once estranged and hostile in mind, doing evil deeds, he has now reconciled in his fleshly body through death, so as to present you holy and blameless and irreproachable before him.'

Individual and corporate

Paul appears to take it for granted that this is an experience, a reality, shared by all believers. It is therefore both an individual experience of entering into Christ, being animated by the Spirit, and a corporate one. Each individual goes down into the waters of baptism as into death, and comes out a changed being, part of a different entity that is composed of all Christians. This entity is new and strange. It does not map simply onto our old lives, and we have to learn how to move in our new form, which necessarily connects us to others.

As many of you as were baptized into Christ have clothed yourselves with Christ. There is no longer Jew or Greek, there is no longer slave or free, there is no longer male and female; for all of you are one in Christ Jesus. (Galatians 3.27–8)

The picture is almost comical, a bit like a gigantic pantomime horse, with everyone inside the skin playing their part invisibly, creating a new character.

The body of Christ

So this notion that we are all 'in Christ' is fundamental to Paul's understanding of church. It is not an opt-in, opt-out society, which you can be part of sometimes and not others. To step 'into' Christ means leaving a life behind. It is gone, dead. Instead, there is a new entity, the body of Christ, free and saved. We do not decide who belongs in this new life, God does. We do not eject people, though we may cut off limbs and cripple the body. Whenever Paul uses this organic description of the community of believers, it is very deliberately to make us think about what disunity does to each one of us, as well as to the whole body.

1 Corinthians 12 is the most extended discussion of the body of Christ, and in it Paul is trying to convey how stupid it is to have hierarchies in the Christian community. If we are a body, we need all the limbs and organs.

> For just as the body is one and has many members, and all the members of the body, though many, are one body, so it is with Christ. For in the one Spirit we were all baptized into one body – Jews or Greeks, slaves or free – and we were all made to drink of one Spirit.
> Indeed, the body does not consist of one member but of many. If the foot were to say, 'Because I am not a hand, I do not belong to the body', that would not make it any less a part of the body . . . Now you are the body of Christ and individually members of it.
> (1 Corinthians 12.12–16, 27. You might like to read the whole of this chapter, and chapter 13, since they belong together.)

The little foot, trying to hop around alone, imagining it has the freedom to decide whether or not it belongs to the body, is the tragicomic Christian who believes that we decide who belongs to our body of Christ. Whereas, in reality, all who eat and drink Christ's body and blood are joined together, like it or not, and can only function together. Ephesians 5.29–30 picks up the same idea. To mistreat each other is as stupid as doing yourself a deliberate injury: 'For no one ever hates his own body, but he nourishes it and tenderly cares for it, just as Christ does for the church.'

It is hard to believe that Paul really meant what he said about this changed entity that we become as we enter the body of Christ. Yet all our sacraments point in the same direction. To be church is to change dramatically. Something has to die for this new life of Christ to be lived. We have to be prepared to let go of some of our rights and needs in order to be part of the body, lived in by the Spirit. It is a glorious new life that is set free in the world, but we are only a small part of it, and we can only operate together with others. On our own, we will be as stupid as the disconnected foot.

Exercise (every body needs exercises)

Read 1 Corinthians 12

1 What is the problem that Paul is trying to combat?
2 Why does 1 Corinthians 13 follow on this chapter?
3 Look at the eucharistic prayer that you are most familiar with, and see what you are asking for when you receive the bread and wine. Here are some examples from *Common Worship*:
4 Prayer A: 'as we eat and drink these holy gifts in the presence of your divine majesty, renew us by your Spirit, inspire us with your love and unite us in the body of your Son'.
5 Prayer B: 'Send the Holy Spirit on your people and gather into one in your kingdom all who share this one bread and one cup.'
6 Prayer D: 'May we and all who share this food offer ourselves to live for you and be welcomed at your feast in heaven, where all creation worships you.'
7 Prayer G: 'As we eat and drink these holy things in your presence, form us in the likeness of Christ, and build us into a living temple to your glory.'

3

Does Church Order Matter?

Most discussion about the Church 'degenerates into disputes about clergy and bishops' (*On Being the Church. Essays on the Christian Community*, ed. C. Gunton and D. Hardy, T. and T. Clark, 1989, p. 49). People say that someone is 'going into the church', meaning that they are going to be ordained. In most ordinary conversation, if 'the church' does not simply mean a building, it means a profession.

The discussions of the last two chapters suggest that that is a sad state to have got into. 'Church' means 'belonging to Jesus', becoming his body, living, united in him, fed by him and filled with his Spirit. But unfortunately, this rapturous state does not do away with the necessity of day-to-day life, and even Acts and Paul's letters are concerned with how to live our lives together so as to give ourselves the best chance of doing and showing what we say we are there for. Church order is designed to facilitate the unity and co-ordination of the body of Christ.

For many people, that suggests that church order is largely functional. It can be changed if it is not doing the job properly, and it might be a good idea to rethink things from time to time. Others think that, on the contrary, few things in Christian living are simply functional. If their function is to enable us and the world to see and believe in the God we worship, then they automatically have a sacred and God-given quality.

Anglican, Roman Catholic and Orthodox churches have bishops, priests and deacons, whose job it is to facilitate worship, learning and mission. This is what is said of each office in the ordination services:

The deacon

- 'Deacons are ordained so that the people of God may be better-equipped to make Christ known. Theirs is a life of visible self-giving. Christ is the pattern of their calling and their commission; as he washed the feet of his disciples, so they must wash the feet of others.'
- 'Deacons are called to work with the Bishop and the priests with whom they serve as heralds of Christ's kingdom. They are to proclaim the gospel in word and deed, as agents of God's purposes of love. They are to serve the community in which they are set, bringing to the Church the needs and hopes of all the people. They are to work with their fellow members in searching out the poor and weak, the sick and lonely and those who are oppressed and powerless, reaching into the forgotten corners of the world, that the love of God may be made visible.'

The service then goes on to describe some of the liturgical functions that the deacon may play.

It sounds as though a deacon is envisaged very much as an outward-facing and practical person, good at working as part of a team, good at noticing the needs of others, and with the kind of shining faith that people find attractive. The service twice uses the word 'visible' of the deacon. They are to be embodying people.

The word 'deacon' is used in a number of contexts in the New Testament. It starts off meaning 'someone who serves', so it is not always clear whether it is being used with formal connotations of ministry or not. Certainly, by the time 1 Timothy is written, it does sound as though Paul's churches have office-holders called 'deacons', whose skills are a mixture of the practical and the spiritual – in fact rather more is said about their spirituality in that letter than that of the bishops. (See 1 Timothy 3.8–10.)

Considering how often Jesus seems to have told his disciples that among his followers, those who serve are the ones who have most understood his own ministry, it is odd that this is the 'order' that the modern church least uses. The ordination service picks up the Gospel reference to Jesus as 'deacon', washing the feet of the disciples, but in practice, deacons have become probationary priests, or people who perform some liturgical functions but not others. Perhaps the time is ripe for a rediscovery of this practical, visible, outward-facing ministry of prayer, evangelism and service.

The priest

The ordination service says this about priests:

- 'Priests are ordained to lead God's people in the offering of praise and the proclamation of the gospel. They share with the Bishop in the oversight of the Church . . . They are to set the example of the Good Shepherd always before them as the pattern of their calling. With the bishop and their fellow presbyters, they are to sustain the community of the faithful by the ministry of word and sacrament.'
- 'Priests are called to be servants and shepherds among the people to whom they are sent. With the Bishop and fellow ministers, they are to proclaim the word of the Lord and to watch for the signs of God's new creation. They are to be messengers, watchmen and stewards of the Lord; they are to teach and to admonish, to feed and provide for his family.'
- The commissioning goes on to speak of preaching, baptizing, expounding the scriptures and presiding at the Lord's table as proper parts of the priestly calling.

Although priests and deacons share some qualities, it does sound as though the priest's job is envisaged as much more concerned with the Christian community, its nurture and growth. There are outgoing aspects to the role, but they are less predominant than in the description of the diaconate. There are also less clearly defined references to the pattern of Christ's own ministry. The main one that the Anglican ordination rite picks up on is that priests are to be like Christ the Good Shepherd, in caring for the flock.

1 Timothy prefers the word 'elders' or 'presbyters' to 'priests', perhaps because 'priests' were a clearly defined group of people in the Old Testament and in Judaism, connected with liturgical sacrifice. Hebrews is firm that this role is now entirely taken on by Christ, and that Christians

have no need of anyone else to perform those kind of functions. What we do continue to need are people to help us live 'in Christ', and this seems to be the focus of priestly ministry, very much centred around the Lord's table, and around the need to build up and guard 'the flock'.

Bishops

- 'Bishops are ordained to be shepherds of Christ's flock and guardians of the faith of the apostles.'
- They are to facilitate, the unity of the body of Christ so that 'formed into a single communion of faith and love, the Church in each place and time is united with the Church in every place and time'.
- Bishops, too, model themselves on the Good Shepherd, though in their case, the image very specifically includes the fact that Jesus, our Good Shepherd, laid down his life for his sheep.
- They are 'principal ministers of word and sacrament', they are responsible for discerning and validating, through ordination, the gifts the Spirit gives for the building up of the Church, and they are to be 'merciful, but with firmness; to minister discipline, but with compassion'.

'Bishop' or *episkopos* means 'someone who has oversight', that is, someone who can see the whole picture. Bishops bring their knowledge of their own local Christian communities to the wider church, and they also bring their knowledge of the wider church to the local. They are to help guard local churches from developing their own personal and idiosyncratic readings of the gospel, but also to help the universal church to remember that the Church is really the whole body of people, trying to live as disciples of Christ, and that all are needed to make up the body of Christ.

Functional or necessary?

Whatever names they might be given, it does seem that the roles undertaken by bishops, priests and deacons are necessary – the outward-facing, the nurturing and the one who holds the local and the universal together. At the time of the Reformation, when the perceived corruption of church structures led many Christians to attempt to go 'back to the New Testament', to find a more authentic expression of church structure, what happened was essentially a re-invention of the wheel. Although officials may have had different titles, they did, in effect, perform much the same kind of function. The one that the Reformed churches were tempted to leave out was the one performed by the bishop, as described above. They wanted to keep the Church much more focused on the actual, local community. This may have been partly in reaction to the way in which the office had been exercised in the past, with many bishops never setting foot in their dioceses, and treating the office purely as a personal power base. But the necessity of connecting the local and the wider church quickly became clear. It is foolish for a community to cut itself off from the resources, in terms of history and experience, of the wider church. It leaves a local church much more open to the possibility of distorting the gospel to fit a particular culture and time, and it also allows a few powerful leaders to dominate, with no obvious wider body to call them to account.

But if we were to conclude that bishops, priests and deacons are good for the Church, that does not mean that the simple and unexamined use of those terms is enough to guarantee good practice. Deacons, in particular, seem to have lost their distinctive role, and how do all of these ordained ministries relate to the ministry exercised by all Christians? This kind of concentration on the particular functions of clergy can make the rest of us feel deskilled and not very necessary. If all these people are our shepherds, are we just the slightly stupid herd, passive and uncontributing? That would not accord well with Paul's picture of the body of Christ, made up of interdependent organs, all vital to the proper functioning of the system. Lay Christians, living and working in 'the world', are the primary ministers of the gospel. The Church discerns, under the guidance of the Holy Spirit, the things we need to help us to function as the body of Christ. But until the gifts brought by ordained Christians are truly seen as just part of the whole variety of things we need to worship and witness to God, 'the church' will remain either a building or a profession, rather than the whole collection of people who belong to the Lord.

Exercise

Read 1 Timothy 3.1–13
1 What do you think of the qualities that are required of bishops and deacons?
2 What qualities do you look for in clergy?
3 If you had to reinvent church order, what would you look for?

4

The Mighty Tortoise Becomes the Body of Christ

The German theologian Wolfhart Pannenberg laid it down as one of the principles of ecclesiology that a theology of the Church must bear some relation to the actual Church we live in. It is very easy to say what a church ought to be like – although there is a surprising amount of disagreement between Christians on the fine detail, even of the theory, let alone the practice of church. But the actual church we inhabit generally bears very little resemblance to this idealized picture. For many people it is the church, not God, that puts them off.

There are good and bad reasons for this. If the church tries to sell itself as the company of those who have the answers and are now living the way we should, then people are right to be sceptical. One glance at the life of any Christian community shows clearly that we are no better than anyone else, and so we are easily accused of hypocrisy. The judgementalism and self-righteousness of many Christian communities, so good at seeing the faults of others, so bad at admitting their own, quite rightly makes people doubt the God to whom we say we are witnessing.

But, on the other hand, there are many people about who want a 'spirituality' without commitment, which makes no demands upon their lives and never asks them not to do what they want to do. That spirituality is not Christianity, and the Christian Church cannot pretend that it is. Many people who met Jesus found him a bit much and intensely disliked what he was saying about God, but he did not change his message to encourage them to follow him under false pretences. Sometimes the

Church puts people off because we are really telling the truth about our God, and people don't like the sound of him.

We can perhaps best distinguish whether we are putting people off for good reasons or bad by concentrating on what we are truly meant to be. Our most basic self-description, as church, is that very simple one – we are people who belong to the Lord. Certain other things must follow from that.

Gratitude, forgiveness and worship

Gratitude should be the most obvious characteristic of the Christian Church. We are the people who know that, although we have done nothing to deserve it, we belong to the Lord. We who were once no people have become God's people; we who had no future now share God's future; we who were once lonely, negligible, useless are now a royal priesthood, a holy nation, with a mission and a purpose and companions to help us along the way.

Along with that gratitude must go humility, because we know that we have achieved nothing. We were not born into the purple, but are wearing borrowed robes that really belong to Jesus. It is surely no accident that the two people on whom the spread of the gospel most depended in the early years after the resurrection are Peter and Paul. The one thing they have in common is their knowledge that they failed Jesus. Peter, after all his boasting, ran away and left Jesus to die alone. Paul hated the Christian gospel, and tried to get rid of it by violence. It is to these men that Jesus commits the mission of the Church. There could hardly be any clearer indication that the foundation of the Church is gratitude. We know our own fallibility, but we also know how much we are trusted. We should be the last people in the world to want to condemn others, because we know that if our God was the condemning kind, we wouldn't be here either.

Christians who convince themselves that they have all the answers and are righteous are, I believe, doing the greatest possible disservice to the mission of the church. We are here to say that if God can forgive us and call us friends, he can do the same with anybody at all.

Out of this gratitude, the worship of the Church is born. Who better to sing God's praises, with our lips and our lives, than us, the ransomed people of God? We know that even our worship is not of our own doing. God the Holy Spirit helps us to pray, begins to draw us into the language of God's people in God's world, otherwise we would not be able to express ourselves. But now we become part of the harmony of the universe that is always flowing, but that we can so seldom hear. We do not create it. It is not as though without our pitiful stumbling there would be no worship of God. But we are fortunate enough to be privileged to join in.

Witness

So the witness of the Church is born out of gratitude and worship. You might not always guess that. Sometimes Christian witness can look as though we are determined that if we can't be happy, neither can anybody else. If we occasionally looked as though we were enjoying ourselves in church, other people might be slightly curious to know why. When we preach, using words if we have to, this is what we are trying to convey – that we are God's grateful people, ransomed, healed, restored, forgiven, brought into a new family, brothers and sisters of Christ, God's heirs, preparing to inherit the world. We are trying to live in the world as though we really believed it belonged to God. But this is not so much a hard grind as a voyage of discovery. We are not judged on our every step. Instead, we learn more and more as we go along, and get given more and more responsibility. Making mistakes, as Peter and Paul found out, often seems to be a passport to something even more challenging.

Nor is our journey a solitary thing. It can't be. Part of what we learn is about our interconnectedness. We are not trying to paint our own picture of the world, with the one or two colours we have at our disposal and our very hazy sense of composition. Instead, we are painting together. What we don't know, someone else will. The colours we can't mix, someone else will have by the bucketful. If we don't want to leave gaping blanks in our canvas, we will need to give everyone a brush, even though that runs the risk that they may have other ideas about what the picture should look like.

So the mission of the Church has this two-fold impetus. We long to share the good news with other people, because we really do think it is the best news ever imaginable, but also because we know that our own understanding of God is incomplete without that of others. The body of Christ is always working at a disadvantage while some of its parts are disconnected.

Implicit in this there should be a certain humility. Christians do believe that Jesus Christ is 'the way, the truth and the life' for everyone. But that does not mean that we have the map, with the whole route clearly planned out. We need the pieces of the journey that others hold. When everybody is 'church', belonging to the Lord, the body of Christ may well look very different from the way we imagined it. Implicit in our mission is a willingness on our part not to be in control, and to allow ourselves to be surprised. Imagine the faces of the Christian Church in Damascus when Ananias ushers in Paul. They all know he has been responsible for the death and imprisonment of any number of Christians, and yet now they have to welcome him and trust him. What's more, as the years go by, they have to hear of him as one of the greatest exponents of the gospel, and see him bringing all kinds of other people into the Christian fellowship. You have to wonder if some of those Damascus Christians wished that their mission had been less successful, and that Paul had never been converted at all, bringing with him all those Gentiles and changing their church for ever. Be careful of mission – you might succeed!

The body of Christ

Gratitude, worship, mission and community are positive and optimistic words, even if what they represent is not achieved easily. But the Church is not just the body of the risen Christ, but also the body of the human, suffering, dying Christ. We have to live with our calling to be despised and rejected, betrayed and mocked. We have to live with the knowledge that if the world did not see Jesus as good news, they certainly are not likely to find us much more attractive. The Church should expect to suffer and even to die in faithful discipleship.

It is easy, particularly for those of us who live in the West, to romanticize this call to suffering. The worst that happens to most of us is a bit of teasing, and perhaps the knowledge that many of our colleagues think we must be soft in the head. There are parts of Christ's body, the Church, that are persecuted and suffering, and it is our duty and our joy to pray for them and speak out for them and do everything we can to show that we are one body, worldwide.

But there are less heroic forms of suffering, too. Christians fighting Christians, despising each other, talking lightly about 'breaking communion', as though our unity is of our making, rather than because we are in Christ, all of this is a different and more shaming kind of suffering. It is tempting to think that no good can come of such suffering, and that all it does is to damage the Church and make it harder for us to witness to our God. It certainly does all that, but with God it is never too late to repent. What we must search for and pray for is some sense, buried deep in our fear and mistrust of other Christians who are not like us, that we can only be the body of Christ if we are together. If, even as we argue and prepare to turn our backs on each other, we can hear Jesus' words to Peter, 'Do you love me?', then perhaps we can begin to trust that we can still be the bearers of God's good news, even though we have betrayed him and inflicted suffering on the 'body of Christ'. Perhaps we may even learn from this suffering, and emerge better equipped to be the church, if only we do not dismember ourselves from the body of Christ.

The body of Christ and the doctrine of the Trinity

In using the metaphor of the body of Christ to describe the Church, Paul is stressing, as hard as he can, that Christians only take meaning from our lives together. This is not surprising, if what we are called to do is to mirror as much as we can see of the nature of our God. God, Father, Son and Holy Spirit is made up of 'persons' in relation. The Father takes his meaning and character from being the Father of the Son. The Son is formed from the Father and makes him visible. The Spirit forms people into the likeness of Christ, so that we can stand in Christ's place and, with the help of the Spirit, call upon God as our Father. Each person of the Trinity delights in being comprehensible only in the context of the others.

We the Church are not yet very much like the Holy Trinity. But we are knit together by the Holy Spirit into the body of Christ. On the cross, Jesus cries out 'My God, my God, why have you forsaken me?', as the full separation of humanity and God falls upon him in death. If the Holy Spirit can hold together Father and Son even in the grave, the Church is not going to be too much of a challenge.

Being the body of Christ means being filled with the life of the Holy Spirit, leading us into obedience to the Father. The work of the Holy Spirit is always to bring the life of Christ, full, abundant and utterly unexpected. We can be confident that life will stream from the body of Christ, even if we are now a part of it.

The Church is not an optional extra to Christianity, but an essential part of it. It does not have to be good, or successful, though that would be nice. It is not ours to make or break, but God's. It is animated by the Holy Spirit, and so long as we still call upon the name of the Father, on the authority of the Son, with the breath of the Holy Spirit, there is hope for us and the world. We should be trying madly to re-member Christ's body, not dis-member it, but in the end, we will not defeat the Spirit of God, any more than death did.

Exercise

1 What do you think puts people off about the Church?
2 Is the church a 'mighty tortoise'? What would you like to see the Church doing?
3 In what ways is your church most faithful/unfaithful to its calling?

5

Exercises

1 The individual in relation to the whole

'Just as every church is a catholic church because the whole of Christ is present in it through the Holy Spirit, so also is every believer a catholic person because the whole Christ dwells in everyone through the Holy Spirit. This understanding of the catholicity of the person not only follows from the qualitative understanding of catholicity, but also draws clear support from biblical statements. Through faith and baptism, every Christian participates in the fullness of the deity dwelling in Jesus Christ (Colossians 2.9–12; cf. John 1.14–16) . . . No Christian, however, can be a catholic person alone, separated from other Christians . . . The issue here is not that the individual must be a member of the overall organism so that the latter can express itself in that member, but rather that if a person is to be catholic, her inner constitution must be determined by an ecclesial community.
(Miroslav Volf, *After our Likeness: The Church as the Image of the Trinity*, Eerdmans, 1998, pp. 279–80).

1 Do you tend instinctively to think of yourself primarily as an individual, or primarily as part of a community?
2 Is it the church that makes you what you are – forms what Volf calls your 'inner constitution'? If not, which relationships do you think do that?
3 What do you understand by this word 'catholic', in relation to the church and to yourself?

2 Your Church

'I think, my dear,' she said, 'the Church used once to be an opiate to you, like that Trebizond enchanter's potion; a kind of euphoric drug. You dramatized it and yourself, you felt carried along in something aesthetically exciting and beautiful and romantic; you were a dilettante, escapist Anglican, I know you read Clement of Alexandria; do you remember where he says, 'We may not be taken up and transported to our journey's end, but must travel thither on foot, traversing the whole distance of the narrow way'? One mustn't lose sight of the hard core, which is, do this, do that, love your friends and like your neighbours, be just, be extravagantly generous, be honest, be tolerant, have courage, have compassion, use your wits and your imagination, understand the world you live in and be on terms with it, don't dramatize and dream of escape. Anyhow, that seems to me to be the pattern, so far as we can make it out here. So come in again with your eyes open, when you feel you can.'
(Rose Macaulay, *The Towers of Trebizond*, Collins, 1956; quoting from 1978 edn, p. 220)

Aunt Dot is speaking to someone who has just been bereaved, and who has not found her faith in God and her relationship with the church to be strong enough to hold her after such a tragedy.

1 If you are a church goer, when did you start and why?
2 Do you feel able to invite others to church?
3 If you had to give an 'eyes open' description of church, what would it be?

3 'Performing the Faith'

Christian faith evokes diverse and sometimes competing images and associations. For some, it conjures up a fairly coherent, albeit complexly interrelated array of experiences, dispositions, attitudes and beliefs. For others faith names not so much the defining subjective features of religious consciousness as the objective content of Christian religion. Faith is thus construed as a set of doctrines, a peculiar body of teaching and instruction. In short, faith is a divine 'deposit' – with the Church of the Bible acting as its repository . . . One of the difficulties of speaking of faith principally in subjective terms, especially in modernity, is that it cuts off Christianity and effectively quarantines it within the narrow, inner realm of the private . . . Likewise, speaking of faith in terms of a deposit induces images and impressions that are at once static and lifeless. Like a meteor fallen to earth, Christian faith objectively understood as 'revealed data' connotes something that is simply 'there' – inert and self-contained because delivered once and for all, intact, whole . . . What is overlooked by both subjective and objective accounts of faith is the sense in which Christian existence is first and foremost an activity – a performance, if you will.

(Stanley Hauerwas, *Performing the Faith*, Brazos Press, 2004, p. 76)

1 Is your description of faith primarily 'subjective' or 'objective'?
2 What do you think the author means by saying that faith is an activity?
3 How might the Church help in the 'performance' of faith?